Trait-Based Writing
Lessons & Activities

■ Kristina Smekens ■

NEW YORK • TORONTO • LONDON • AUCKLAND • SYDNEY

MEXICO CITY • NEW DELHI • HONG KONG • BUENOS AIRES

Teaching *Resources*

DEDICATION

To the thousands of students who helped shape each of these mini-lessons within classroom models around the country.

To the teachers who love to teach writing . . . and to those who are learning to love it.

Contributors:
Stacey Callahan, *St. Joseph–St. Elizabeth School (Ft. Wayne, IN)*
David Henry, *Sweetser Elementary (Sweetser, IN)*
Claudia Jackson, *Wilbur Wright Elementary (New Castle, IN)*
Barb Katenkamp, *North Dearborn Elementary (Guilford, IN)*
Mary Kiningham, *Cedarville Elementary (Ft. Wayne, IN)*
Staci Salzbrenner, *Woodburn Elementary (Woodburn, IN)*

Acquiring Editor: Virginia Dooley
Editor: Sarah Glasscock
Copyeditor: Eileen Judge
Cover design: Ka-Yeon Kim-Li
Interior design: Melinda Belter
Illustrations: Kristina Smekens

ISBN-13: 978-0-545-09659-1
ISBN-10: 0-545-09659-6
Copyright © 2009 by Kristina Smekens.

All rights reserved. Published by Scholastic.
Printed in the U.S.A.

1 2 3 4 5 6 7 8 9 10   40   15 14 13 12 11 10 09

Contents

Introduction

I remember the day my sixth-grade teacher stood in front of class and taught us about the essay introduction. I can still hear her voice in my head: "Class, an introduction is the first paragraph of your writing. It is where you grab the attention of the reader and explain what your essay is all about." After that brief explanation, she stood at the board with her chalk poised and said, "Now, who would like to try one?"

What?! What does she want us to do? What is an introduction again? I was frantic. I didn't raise my hand. I stopped making eye contact with the teacher. I had no idea what she was talking about. I looked around the room, and it was obvious no one else did either. That's when it happened. She called on me: "Kristina? What do you think? How about you try to write an introduction?" My response was what I assume would be any other sixth grader's response: "I didn't have my hand up."

Here's what I have since realized. I couldn't write an introduction because I'd never seen a good introduction. I couldn't write an introduction, because my teacher didn't tell me *how* to write one. Writing used to be about the topic (the ideas you wrote about) and the conventions (how correct the writing was). However, writing instruction has evolved to be more about *how* to weave those traits and others into a well-constructed piece. And if *you* never learned how to write, it's difficult to be the "expert" in the room teaching a classroom of students.

That said, I wanted to create a book of mini-lessons that focused on *how* to teach individual writing skills for each of the six traits of writing—ideas, organization, voice, word choice, sentence fluency, and conventions. But my next step was to determine which skills to target. I went searching for the writing weaknesses that most often plague intermediate student writing. I identified numerous problem areas and then whittled the list down to the top 20. If my assumption is correct, many or all of the following writing weaknesses are plaguing your students' writing, too.

1. Writing is too broad and unfocused.

2. Writing lacks development.

3. Writing lacks specific details.

4. Peer revision isn't producing improved content.

5. Prewrites include whole sentences.

6. Writing lacks a beginning and/or an ending.

7. Middles (the body) aren't developed enough.

8. Transitions are too simplistic.

9. Writing lacks voice.

10. Writing lacks voice-filled words and phrases.

11. Writing lacks a sense of audience.

12. Writing lacks vivid vocabulary.

13. Writing lacks precise word choice.

14. Writing uses predictable word choice.

15. Writing lacks strong action verbs.

16. Writing lacks and/or misuses punctuation.

17. Sentences are generally the same length.

18. Sentences don't flow smoothly from one to the next.

19. Writer isn't editing for punctuation marks.

20. Writer isn't self-editing intensely.

This book provides 20 practical mini-lessons that specifically address these writing weaknesses. Each mini-lesson includes focused instruction with student writing samples and suggestions for ways to demonstrate the skill and provide follow-up writing experiences. Here's a quick reference list:

WRITING/WRITER WEAKNESS	MINI-LESSON TITLE
Writing is too broad and unfocused	**Narrow the Topic**
Writing lacks development	**ABC Detail Chart**
Writing lacks specific details	**Pump-Up the Details**
Peer revision isn't producing improved content	**Revising Ideas**
Prewrites include whole sentences	**Grocery-List Prewriting**
Writing lacks a beginning and/or an ending	**Tie Beginning to Ending**
Middles (the body) aren't developed enough	**Develop the Middle**
Transitions are too simplistic	**Transition Sentences**
Writing lacks voice	**Hearing Voice**
Writing lacks voice-filled words and phrases	**Finding Voice**
Writing lacks a sense of audience	**"Test Lady" Audience**
Writing lacks vivid vocabulary	**Purple Words**
Writing lacks precise word choice	**Shades of Words**
Writing uses predictable word choice	**Taboo Words**
Writing lacks strong action verbs	**Dead Verbs**
Writing lacks punctuation and/or misuses punctuation	**Hearing Punctuation**
Sentences are generally the same length	**Slinky Sentences**
Sentences don't flow smoothly from one to the next	**Sentence Length for Impact**
Writer isn't editing for punctuation marks	**Punctuation Walkabout**
Writer isn't self-editing intensely	**Read Up, Write Down**

So will there still be writing weaknesses after executing these 20 lessons? Sure. This book won't "fix" all your writers. In fact, this isn't a resource with *the* six-trait lessons for intermediate teachers. There is no such thing. There is no set of six-trait lessons. You undoubtedly have dozens of lessons that target these and other writing weaknesses, and the lessons work well. The notion isn't to purge those lessons in exchange for these. Rather, use these mini-lessons as additional ways to address problematic writer weaknesses. When you are looking for a new way to address the same writing issue, this resource might be just the answer.

1 *Trait Connection:* **Ideas**

Narrow the Topic

LESSON RATIONALE

When writing topics are too broad, students will simply skim the surface, listing general idea after general idea. To encourage students to develop their ideas and add details, you need to teach them how to work from a small and manageable topic—a narrow topic.

LESSON TRIGGER

This lesson will reveal how to take a big topic and make it small. It's easier to elaborate on ideas and write with more specific detail when the topic is narrowly focused. Before teaching the mini-lesson, look for objects that shrink or nest, such as nesting boxes or varying sizes of envelopes or gift bags. Label each as shown in the photo on page 8 and use them to walk the class through this process of narrowing a broad topic.

Mini-Lesson

Display a broad and undeveloped piece of writing like the "Halloween" writing sample below.

> HALLOWEEN
>
> Halloween is my favorite holiday because I get to go trick-or-treating. I get a lot of candy every year. One time I was a ballerina and wore a crown. Another year I dressed up like a clown. I had red-and-white clown makeup on my face. It was very messy.

Ask students to identify all the topics listed in the story (Halloween, trick-or-treating, candy, costumes, ballerina, clown, and so on). Because the topic of Halloween is too large, the writer just lists ideas without developing them. In order to narrow the topic, he or she must zoom in and focus on one idea, like trick-or-treating.

Display the nesting objects for the topic of Halloween and reveal the "Trick-or-Treating" box. Point out that just because the topic of trick-or-treating is smaller than Halloween doesn't mean it's narrow enough. With trick-or-treating, the writer could write about costumes, candy, the neighborhood, the weather, and so on. Again, the writer needs to select a smaller idea. Reveal the nesting box labeled "Costumes."

Question students about what they think of this topic. Is it small and narrow enough, or is it still a little too broad? Unless the writer focuses on one costume, he or she might list different outfits—still just a string of topics. The writer should consider narrowing it down to a single costume, like a clown costume.

Reveal the nesting box labeled "Clown." Or, further narrow the topic down to a single component of a clown costume, the make-up. In that case, reveal the final nested box, "Clown Make-up" and display the "My Clown Face" writing sample.

Nesting boxes show how to narrow the topic of Halloween.

MY CLOWN FACE

Halloween is my favorite holiday because I get to dress up in fun costumes and wear make-up. When I was little, I was a clown. I had an outfit with colored polka dots. It had a funny hat with bells and big, red clown shoes.

The best part of the whole costume was my make-up. My brother smeared white face paint all over my forehead, nose, and chin. Then he put two huge red circles on my cheeks, and a big red smile on my lips. My eyes were painted like black triangles, and my nose had a puffy, blue ball on it.

I had so much make-up on my face that I couldn't wash it all off that night! The next day at school, I still had light-red circles stained on my cheeks.

Continue to reinforce the concept of a topic shrinking. Work with the class to take large topics (e.g., school, family, friends) and narrow them to smaller, more focused ideas. See the graphic at the right with "school" narrowed down to "the game winning run of a kickball game."

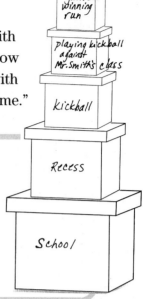

INDEPENDENT STUDENT WRITING ACTIVITY

After the class has practiced narrowing topics, move students into small groups or pairs to continue experimenting. Have them use the reproducible on page 10 to narrow down topics such as chores, field trips, sports, hobbies, and animals.

GROUP SHARE

Have each group/pair share its favorite small topic with the class. Ask students to describe how they narrowed the topic. Discuss how they made decisions as to which smaller topics to pursue and which to abandon. Question students about what they will remember about this lesson when starting their next pieces.

LESSON **EXTENSION**

Students have learned to narrow down big topics to smaller ones. The next step is for them to prewrite the specific details for the smaller, narrower topic. The example below narrows the enormous topic of summer down to just one aspect—surviving the long drive to the beach. The relevant details for the topic are brainstormed during the prewriting stage. These details will become the meat of the first draft. Be sure students understand that narrowing the topic does not replace the prewriting step of the writing process.

After walking students through the example, have them use the reproducible on page 11 to brainstorm details for the topic they thought of in their group.

NOTE Be mindful that you can make a topic too small. When that happens, the writer can't manage to develop more than one or two sentences.

LESSON 1: NARROW THE TOPIC

Name _____ Date _____

Narrow the Topic

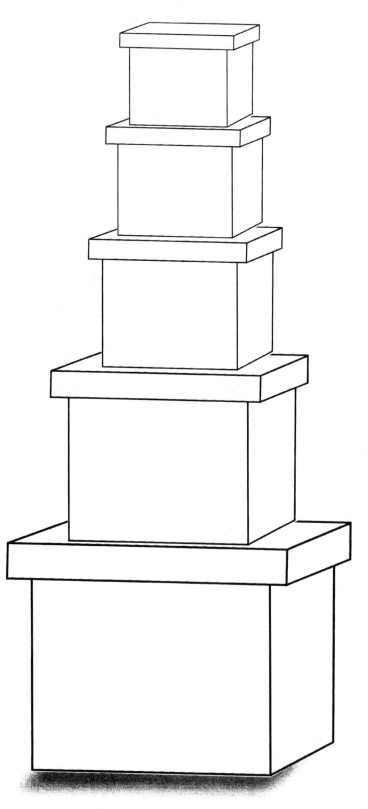

Trait-Based Writing: Lessons and Activities © 2009 by Kristina Smekens, Scholastic Teaching Resources

Name _____ Date _____

Adding Details to the Topic

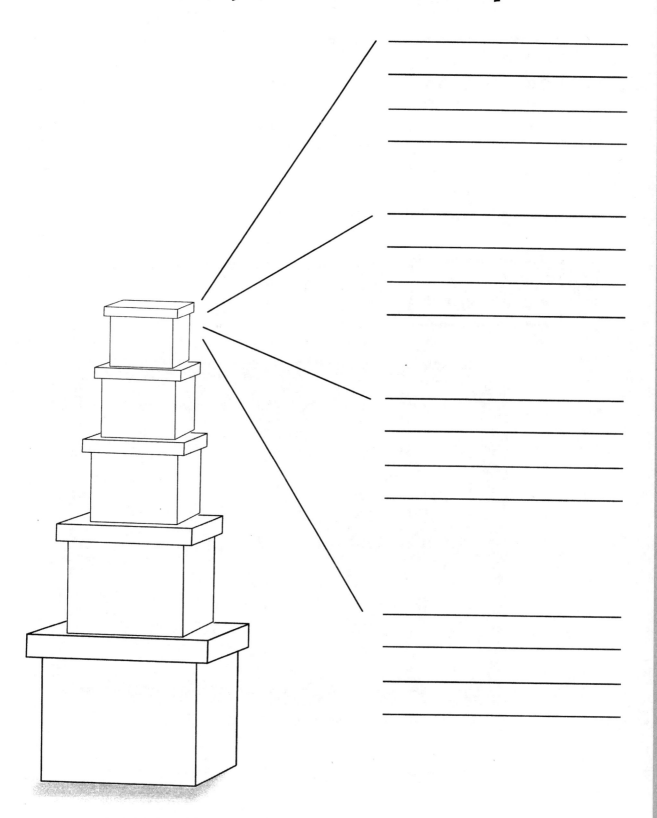

ABC Detail Chart

LESSON RATIONALE

It is common practice for students to brainstorm or prewrite with a graphic organizer (i.e., a planning web or beginning/middle/end). However, for many students the process of completing a graphic organizer can be confusing. Some students struggle with filling it out or organizing details. Others write complete sentences on the pre-write page—not realizing the purpose of the prewrite is to list details.

With this lesson, students are not required to fill out a form. Instead, they are asked to randomly list every detail they know about a topic. Initially, these details will be sorted and organized based on the first letter of the detail.

LESSON TRIGGER

Display a large ABC chart that has room in the center to record the writing topic.

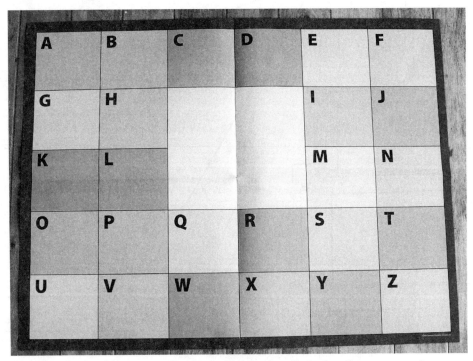

ABC Chart (published by Smekens Education Solutions)

Mini-Lesson

Identify a current content-area topic (e.g., plants), a current literature theme (e.g., revenge), or a timely seasonal topic (e.g., sledding). Tell students that if you asked them to write about plants (or any timely topic you've been studying), you might get information as skimpy as the following:

> Plants have leaves, roots, stems, and stuff. They need food and water to grow. There are lots of different kinds of plants. That's all I know. I hope you liked it. The End.

After the predictable giggles from students, remind them that they've studied this topic for multiple days and, consequently, the information and details in their writing on this topic should be abundant. To help them crank out details *before* they write, introduce them to the ABC Detail Chart.

Write the topic on a large sticky note and place it in the center of the chart. Then ask students to begin recalling what they've learned about the topic. Write each detail or fact they mention on a sticky note and adhere it to the chart, based on the first letter of the word/phrase.

Continue to prompt students with facets of the subject matter they haven't tapped yet, for example: *What is a plant's growing cycle? What do plants need to grow? What are the parts of a plant?* (You can also use this as an opportunity to review key vocabulary.)

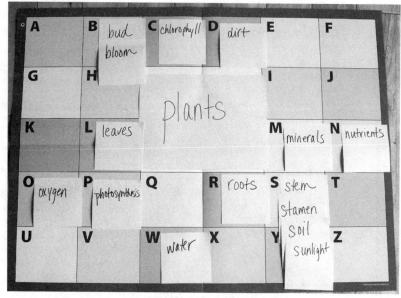

The topic of this ABC Detail Chart is plants.

LESSON 2: ABC DETAIL CHART

INDEPENDENT STUDENT WRITING ACTIVITY

Have small groups complete another ABC Details Chart for a second topic. Challenge the groups to see which can brainstorm the most sticky-note details on the given topic.

GROUP SHARE

Ask students to share how using the ABC format helped their prewriting. Showcase one or two good prewriting examples to share with the class. Point out that their drafts will be more thorough and organized with the use of the ABC Detail Chart.

LESSON EXTENSION

If you utilized sticky notes for each letter on the ABC Chart, students can pull them off and group them into categories based on commonalities. Without organizing the sticky note details, students tend to write an alphabetical list of sentences about the topic. By sorting and grouping the details, they are organizing information and beginning to form their paragraphs.

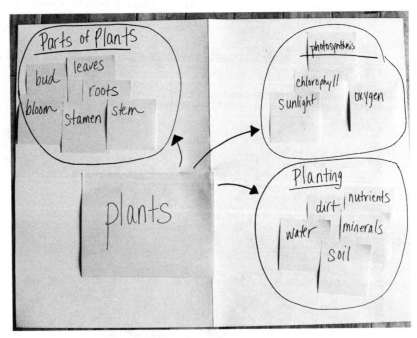

Sticky notes grouped into categories.

TRAIT-BASED WRITING

Pump-Up the Details

LESSON RATIONALE

Do you find yourself always encouraging your students to add more details and make their writing longer? This lesson demonstrates the idea of pumping up their writing with limitless details. For some students, this is just the hook they need to end skimpy writing.

LESSON TRIGGER

Kids associate the concept of "pumping-up" with the inflating of a balloon. It makes a great analogy for expanding a writer's ideas.

Mini-Lesson

To introduce the idea of pumping-up details, start with a simple piece of writing no longer than a couple of sentences.

> This weekend, I took my dog for a walk. We went far. It was fun.

Describe this initial draft as deflated and lacking detail, and show students a deflated balloon. Ask them to add some details to "pump-up" the dog-walking story you've started. For example, a student might say, "We went to the park." For every added sentence, breathe a puff of air into the balloon.

> This weekend, I took my dog Barney for a walk. We went far. It was fun. We went to the park. I carried him up the slide. Then, we went down together. I rode behind, as he barked all the way down.

By this time, the balloon you're inflating will be pretty big. However, keep adding sentences until you observe a student cover his or her ears or comment that it's about to pop. That's when you've got them! Respond by saying, "Are you afraid this balloon is going to pop? I forgot to tell you. This is not an ordinary balloon. This is a Writer's Balloon. It's unpoppable! You can never add too many details."

NOTE Obviously, you are blowing up an ordinary balloon, and it definitely could pop! So, as you practice "pumping-up" writing with students, be careful not to overinflate the balloon.

Continue this process of adding detail sentences aloud. There is no sense in moving students to writing on paper until they can develop their ideas orally. Let the air out of the balloon, and "pump-up" another skimpy sample as shown below.

Original

I'm glad recess is over. It is freezing out there.

Pumping It Up

I'm glad recess is over. It is freezing out there. <u>It started snowing after we got out there.</u>

I'm glad recess is over. It is freezing out there. It started snowing after we got out there. <u>The snow was coming down quickly.</u>

I'm glad recess is over. It is freezing out there. It started snowing after we got out there. The snow was coming down quickly. <u>Everyone was covered in white.</u>

I'm glad recess is over. It is freezing out there. It started snowing after we got out there. The snow was coming down quickly. Everyone was covered in white. <u>When the bell finally rang, we all dashed inside.</u>

For additional practice with this skill, you might ask students to look through their most recent writing and find a piece of "deflated writing" that needs pumping-up. Work as a class to do just that.

INDEPENDENT STUDENT WRITING ACTIVITY

Have students look through their recent writing again for some additional "deflated" sentences or complete pieces that need pumping-up. Give them an opportunity to go back and see how many pumped-up sentences they can add using colored pens.

GROUP SHARE

Call on volunteers to first read their initial pencil drafts, and then their colored-pen revisions. As they read aloud, blow up a balloon to represent how much "bigger" the writing is now, compared to their originals.

LESSON EXTENSION

Provide students with four specific ways to "pump-up" their writing by including the following types of details:

1. **Number Details:** date, time, temperature, length, width, weight, height, age, quantity, speed, and so on

2. **Name Details:** person's name, animal/pet name, month, season, city, state, street, breed, brand name, and so on

3. **Comparison Details:** similes, metaphors, analogies, and so on

4. **Sensory Details:** sights, sounds, smells, tastes, textures

These four strategies can be applied to the winter recess sample in the mini-lesson.

Adding NUMBER & NAME details:

I'm glad recess is over. It is freezing out there. It started snowing after we got out there <u>at 11:15 A.M. The recess monitor, Mrs. Brown, said it was 17 degrees.</u>

Adding COMPARISON details:

I'm glad recess is over. It is freezing out there. It started snowing after we got out there at 11:15 A.M. The recess monitor, Mrs. Brown, said it was 17 degrees. <u>Everyone looked like they had white wigs on their heads.</u>

Adding SENSORY details:

I'm glad recess is over. It is freezing out there. <u>Every time I breathed in through my nose, I could feel little icicles forming in my nostrils</u>. It started snowing after we got out there at 11:15 A.M. The recess monitor, Mrs. Brown, said it was 17 degrees. Everyone looked like they had white wigs on their heads.

Revising Ideas

LESSON RATIONALE

When students peer revise, the outcome typically has the partner declaring, "It's good. It's fine. I like it." To offset this unproductive conversation, teachers often announce that each partner must give the student-writer three ideas to improve the draft. This frequently leads to minor changes (e.g., simple word substitutions, small detail additions, or editing corrections in spelling and punctuation). Again, none of these really strengthen the content of the writing.

To encourage serious reflection and an overhaul of writing, base the peer-revision conversation around four big questions.

LESSON TRIGGER

Revision Conferencing Cards, along with the four symbols, are great tools to support this lesson.

Revision Conferencing Cards (published by Smekens Education Solutions)

Mini-Lesson

Discuss students' experiences with peer revision conferences. Explain that today's mini-lesson will help them structure the conversation between the writer and his or her reader. It will accomplish this by providing stronger feedback for a writer. Introduce students to the following four big questions:

1. What's the best part of the writing?

2. What do you (the reader) want to know more about?

3. What is fuzzy (awkward or confusing) to you, the reader?

4. What do you want less of (word, phrase, idea, off-topic sentence)?

Reveal a first-draft writing sample, such as the letter below, as students follow along.

Dear Mom and Dad,

    I would love to get Internet. I promise I will NOT break the rules you make. If I do, you can take the computer away. If Kristen and Kyle break the rules you can do whatever!

    Also, when we go camping, we can look up campsites on the Internet. We can get hotels off the Internet, too.

    The best way it to help us with projects. It can help us with science and social studies projects. Mom, Dad, please concern it.

                Love,

                Megan

    P.S. We can play educational games, and Mom you can
        buy antiques off EBay, too.

    P.P.S. I guess I can help around the house too.

When you're finished reading, ask: "What's the best part?" (Other variations of "best" might include the following: "What part is so good you wish you'd written it? What's the word, phrase, sentence, or idea that you will remember because it is so good? What do you think the writer should leave alone because it's already so good?" Indicate students' responses about the best part of the letter with a star.

Next, ask: "What do you want to know more about?" (Variations include the following: "What did the writer mention, but not fully develop? What parts do you think are the most interesting and could use more details? Is there a part you wish would 'come to life' with more sensory description?" Indicate the places that students feel need more elaboration with a plus sign.

Continue with the third question: "What's fuzzy or confusing?" (Variations include the following: "What parts make you go 'huh'? What doesn't make sense? Where did you get lost? What sentences sound awkward?" Indicate the sections that were unclear to students with a question mark.

And finally, ask: "What should be cut? Not everything this writer included is great. Suggest he take out some parts that are irrelevant or off topic. Or, maybe he overused a word and needs to come up with a synonym. Or, maybe a part goes on and on, and you think the writer should remove some of the information to make it move faster." Indicate sections that students think should be cut with a minus sign.

Here's a run down of how a fourth-grade class responded to the sample on page 21:

 The class thought that offering a punishment for breaking the rules would appeal to the parents. The star in the first paragraph indicates to the writer that this is a "good part."

 The class suggested the writer explain *how* the Internet could help in finding campsites. Notice a second plus sign; the students suggested the writer elaborate on how the Internet could help with school projects.

TRAIT-BASED WRITING

? The class identified two instances of awkward phrasing. The following wording in the first sentence doesn't make sense: "The best way it to help us with projects." The writer appears to have left out a word, making it confusing for the reader. Within the same paragraph, the writer ends with "please concern it." The class suggested it might be the wrong word. A third fuzzy spot is marked within the final P.P.S. of the letter. The reader is confused about the relevancy of persuading parents for the Internet and helping around the house. This idea needs to be tied to the main idea more directly. It seems out of place right now.

— The opening line of the letter could be cut. The class thought it was too obvious, too pushy. Students suggested replacing it with a more subtle and persuasive hook.

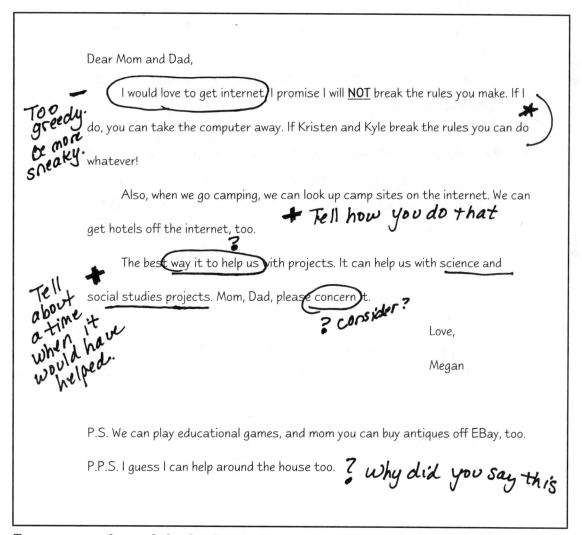

To accompany the symbols, the class included specific comments.

LESSON 4: REVISING IDEAS

The writer then uses the reader's feedback to springboard into revision. However, it's the writer who decides how best to improve the draft. This keeps the ownership of the writing in the hands of the author. A writer does not need to take every suggestion and make every change. Reveal the revised draft to students.

Dear Mom and Dad,

Do you think we should get Internet? I do, and here are some reasons why. I promise I will NOT break the rules you make. If I do, you can take the computer away. If Kristen and Kyle break the rules you can do whatever!

Also, when we go camping, you know we can't always find or get campsites. Well we can look and reserve campsites on the Internet. We can reserve hotels off the Internet, too.

The best part is that it helps us with projects. You know that we almost always need the Internet for our science and social studies projects. You know it is a waste of gas to go to Debbie's house to use the Internet. Mom, Dad, please consider it.

Love,
Megan

P.S. We can play educational games, and Mom you can purchase antiques off EBay, too.

P.P.S. I guess I can help around the house, too, if that will help you say yes.

INDEPENDENT STUDENT WRITING ACTIVITY

Identify a current draft for each student to revisit. Have them work with a partner or within a small group. Each student-writer will read aloud his or her draft. Then, the other student(s) will answer each of the four big questions about the writer's draft. Continue until each student has had a chance to read and have his or her work critiqued. After the peer conferences, students should begin making revisions to their drafts.

GROUP SHARE

Have students reveal an original sentence or a portion of their drafts and the revisions they made based on reader feedback.

LESSON EXTENSION

The goal of revision is to make a piece of writing sound better, clearer, and more thorough. Revision shouldn't be about rewriting or recopying. Teach students ways to create space within a draft so they can add, change, and cut content without recopying.

1. When a word, phrase, or sentence needs to be deleted, teach students to **strikethrough**. Blackening the portion so much so that it's unreadable creates

> Mom, Dad, please ~~concern~~ consider it.

a messy-looking draft. Moreover, students often cross out portions of the writing that, in the end, they want to reuse somewhere else. If it's unreadable, then the writer needs to craft the idea all over again. Teach them to draw a single line through the text, to strikethrough.

2. When a word or two needs to be added, teach students to use the **caret** to insert details. Details can be written above the caret or in the margins.

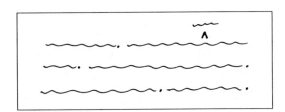

3. If a student wants to add in a sentence or two, then **spider legs** is a perfect technique to use. After writing the sentence(s) on a strip of paper (a "leg"), the writer tapes it onto the "body" of the piece where he or she wants to insert it.

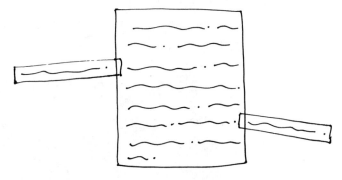

4. The student who doesn't want anything "dangling" off his or her paper can simply write the additional sentence at the bottom of the page and indicate where to move it with a **circle and arrow.**

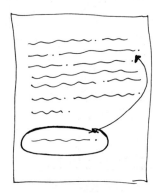

5. When a writer needs to add larger chunks of text (multiple sentences), spider legs won't provide enough space. Suggest **story surgery**. This is when the writer cuts apart a story (at the point where he or she wants to insert an additional paragraph) and tapes in another sheet of paper. Compare story surgery to "cutting open the story," "messing with the guts," and "adding an organ."

Many students love watching their writing physically grow in length.

This technique also works well when a writer needs to rearrange the order of ideas and sentences. Simply have him or her cut apart each idea and tape them back together in a more appropriate sequence.

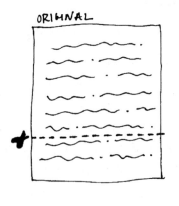

ORIHNAL

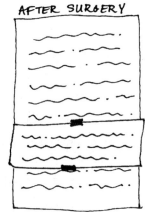

AFTER SURGERY

6. For the student who needs to add a chunk of text but doesn't want the mess of story surgery, suggest creating an **inserts page**. This requires another sheet of paper. Within the draft, the writer indicates with an endnote symbol where he or she wants to add more. Then, using the same symbol on the inserts page, the writer drafts the additional sentences.

NOTE All writers are different. Some love the tools mentioned above and are motivated to revise because it's fun. Other students prefer their writing to stay neat and tidy, even during the revision stage. Be sure to offer students a variety of ways to re-enter a draft to revise and strengthen it.

Grocery-List Prewriting

When planning or organizing anything in life, most people would acknowledge that they make a list (e.g., grocery items, errands, to do's, action steps, note taking, and so on). In turn, many student writers work better from a list, rather than from formal graphic organizers, such as a web, Venn diagram, or beginning/middle/end. Teach them prewriting strategies for developing thorough and organized lists of details.

LESSON TRIGGER

Consider using shopping list or "To Do" list paper for this lesson. The long, vertical format encourages students to use itemized words and phrases in a prewrite rather than complete sentences.

Mini-Lesson

Describe the contents of a grocery list and how such lists are written. Some of your points might include the following:

- Grocery lists are written for the shopper; no one else reads them.
- Grocery lists contain single words *(ketchup)* versus complete sentences *(The red ketchup bottle has a white label)*.
- Abbreviations are used when appropriate; correct spelling is not essential *(TP = toilet paper)*.

Draw the following comparison between the characteristics of a grocery shopping list and a prewriting list:

- A prewrite is created by and read by the writer only.
- Ideas are written in words and phrases—not in complete sentences.

• Abbreviations are used when appropriate; correct spelling is not a concern.

Pass out a sheet of shopping list paper for each student. Challenge the class to list all the facts, details, and information they know about a particular topic.

In the sample at the right, notice that the details are written in words and phrases. The only goal at this point is to create a thorough list. Make sure all the students are creating identical lists and using only words and phrases—no sentences.

Now that the lists are done, teach students how to organize them by again drawing on the grocery store analogy. Ask: "Have you ever been to the store with your parent who was shopping from a list, and you found yourself backtracking among the aisles? That's because the shopper didn't organize the list! Who can tell me the organization of a grocery store?" (e.g., produce, meat, frozen, dairy, and so on) "Now, it's time to organize your prewriting list." Have students use numbers to group details in their lists that go together.

This prewriting strategy targets both the traits of ideas and organization. It helps the writer determine what details go together and how to group ideas (paragraphs) while writing the first draft. Without this second step, writing will jump around from detail to detail, frustrating the reader.

NOTE A more visual strategy for organizing the prewriting list might be to color code the details using highlighters.

pink: all about leaves

yellow: all about fall weather

orange: all about fall holidays

green: all about activities and sports played in the fall

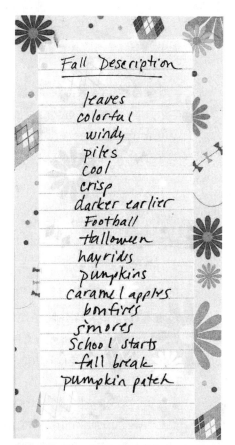

Description of fall on shopping list paper

Details grouped in categories and numbered

LESSON 5: GROCERY-LIST PREWRITING

INDEPENDENT STUDENT WRITING ACTIVITY

Consider creating grocery-list prewrites for several different topics. Provide students with multiple sheets of shopping list paper and have them work to **1**) create grocery lists of details, and **2**) organize those details into groups.

NOTE Students do not write any first drafts with these lists. The purpose of this mini-lesson and subsequent writing time is to give them experience in creating strong "grocery lists" of details.

GROUP SHARE

Wrap up with a class discussion. Ask students what they like about grocery-list pre-writing, and how it is different than other prewriting strategies they have used before. Be sure also to mention that as helpful as a grocery list is for a shopper, it doesn't do any good if he or she leaves the list at home. The point is that when students transition from prewriting to the first draft, they should reference the grocery list of details while writing. Some shoppers literally cross items off their list when they put each one in their carts. Your writers might benefit from a similar approach. After including a detail in their pieces, students could cross it off their prewrite lists. Without the list, the writer tends to add extra (off-topic) sentences or forget important ideas.

LESSON EXTENSION

In future mini-lessons, extend the prewriting skills to include a focus on action verbs. Review the list of words and details brainstormed about the topic of fall and notice how it is predominantly composed of adjectives and nouns. By thinking of verbs, too, the sentences within the draft will be stronger: *harvesting, carving, jumping, raking, burning, trick-or-treating, roasting,* and so on.

Tie Beginning to Ending

**L E S S O N
RATIONALE**

One of the characteristics of strong writing is that it reads as a cohesive whole—meaning it includes a beginning, middle, and end. Since most students write pretty good "middles," target beginnings and endings as a single unit. This tends to produce an opening and closing that work well together.

**L E S S O N
T R I G G E R**

Show students that story structure is like the motion of a yo-yo; the beginning and ending work together. Releasing the yo-yo represents the beginning. The spinning at the bottom of the string represents the middle. And the yo-yo spiraling back up to the user's hand represents the ending.

Most student-writers release the yo-yo (beginning) and let it spin (middle), but they often neglect to bring it back up for the reader (ending). Consequently, the piece stops at the end of the middle or just includes a canned one-liner like "The End" or "That's all I know. Hope you liked my story," or "Good-bye," or "Thank you for reading this."

Mini-Lesson

This lesson offers students a structure for creating beginnings and endings. As mentioned in the Lesson Trigger, think of structure as a yo-yo. However a piece begins (send down the yo-yo), it can end the same way (bring the yo-yo back up). For example, if the writing begins with action, it can end with action. If it starts with a sound effect, it can end with a sound effect. If it begins with sensory description, then it can end with sensory description.

Share the following example of a middle about a bike wreck with students:

> I was riding faster and faster. Then, all of a sudden, my wheel hit a pothole and I went flying. End over end I somersaulted in the air. When I touched down again, I didn't just crash. I slid. I skidded. I skimmed across the road. When I came to a stop, my elbows and knees were bleeding. My hands hurt.

Using this same "middle" over and over, orally recite several different story beginnings and endings while the students listen. Some examples appear below.

NOTE You don't need many details about the bike wreck itself because the "middle" isn't the important part of this lesson. The key is that students hear patterned beginnings and endings.

1. INTENSE ACTION

Beginning: I was pedaling fast down Hicker Hill on my brand new bike. My legs were going around and around. I remember picking up speed with every rotation.

Middle: the wreck

Ending: It took a long time to hobble back up the hill, hauling my bike parts. There was a throbbing pain in my palms. They were scraped and raw, with speckles of gravel buried in them. Man, did they burn!

2. SENSORY DESCRIPTION

Beginning: My new bike reflected the sunshine; it bounced off the shiny chrome trim. There was a white plastic basket with seven dainty purple flowers on the front. I swung my leg over it and began my first ride.

Middle: the wreck

Ending: But no matter how banged up I was, you should have seen my not-so-new bike. The chrome was dented. The paint was chipped. The basket was dangling from the handlebars, with only one purple flower remaining.

TRAIT-BASED WRITING

3. INTRIGUING QUESTION

Beginning: Have you ever felt like you were flying? I have—the day I zoomed down Hicker Hill on my brand-new bike.

Middle: the wreck

Ending: Well, you've seen a bird fly and crash into a window before, haven't you?

4. MOOD-SETTING EMOTION

Beginning: What a great day for bike riding! The sun was shining. The air was crisp. I was ready to hit the road, just me and my new bike.

Middle: the wreck

Ending: It all went wrong, terribly wrong. All I want to do now is dump this bike in the garage and forget this day forever.

5. SOUND EFFECT/ONOMATOPOEIA

Beginning: WHIZ! The trees were behind me. WHIZ! I zoomed past a parked car. WHIZ! WHIZ! WHIZ! I passed mailboxes one by one. No one could catch me on my brand-new bike.

Middle: the wreck

Ending: CLINK! CLANK! CLUNK! The chain from my bike rhythmically banged against the bent fender as I hauled my once-new bike back to the house. CLINK! CLANK! CLUNK!

Continue creating combinations of beginnings and endings. The possibilities are endless.

INDEPENDENT STUDENT WRITING ACTIVITY

Reveal "The Biggest Snowball Fight" writing sample on page 32. The beginning/ending combination utilizes the intense action strategy.

Have pairs use the same "middle" paragraphs to develop another type of beginning/ending combination (sensory description, mood-setting emotion, intriguing question, or sound effect).

LESSON 6: TIE BEGINNING TO ENDING

THE BIGGEST SNOWBALL FIGHT!

Intense Action beginning ▶ WHAM! Cold, frozen ice chips slammed into my face. Whoa . . . ? What's going on . . . ? It wasn't until I wiped the snow off my eyelids and fluttered my eyelashes that I saw them.

Middle ▶ It was the local neighborhood army. They looked like a fleet of a thousand or more kids. I didn't even recognize most of them, but this wasn't the time for introductions.

I dived into the house and gathered my defense. They broke my window while I was in there. So I got my brother in this because he is the champ at throwing snowballs. Also because he's 13.

So we gathered snowballs in the front yard. When the pile was huge, we loaded it into the wagon and slowly pulled it to the backyard. When we got there, we fired one ball after another at all those kids. We threw them faster than they could make them. And when they ran away from us, we pulled the wagon and chased them down.

Intense Action ending ▶ Out of breath, we doubled over and panted. We shook our gloved fists in victory. AAAHHHHH! Two against a thousand . . . and we still won!

GROUP SHARE

Ask pairs to read aloud their combinations of beginnings and endings. See if the class can determine the type they utilized.

LESSON EXTENSION

As a class, look through picture books or literature examples for additional ways to start and end writing. Maintain a list of examples, including excerpts. These can be collected on a wall chart, or students can keep them in their writers' notebooks.

Trait Connection: Organization

Develop the Middle

LESSON RATIONALE

The traditional Beginning/Middle/End (BME) graphic organizer is a common starting point for prewriting. It encourages students to remember all three components of a complete piece. However, it can also limit idea development. With only one middle box, students don't effectively plan out the body of their writing. To help them develop the middle even more, consider converting the simple BME organizer to a more thorough storyboard (the 9-grid format discussed on page 34). This prewriting concept merges quick sketches with key words, all organized within sequenced frames.

LESSON TRIGGER

Teach students to s-t-r-e-t-c-h the middle of their stories by comparing it to a train. Consider the beginning as the engine, and the ending as the caboose. This lesson teaches students to write more by adding more middle sentences, more middle cars.

Mini-Lesson

As a class, study the BME prewrite and the first draft of "Making a Pie" shown below.

MAKING A PIE

I was going to help my mom make a pie. We drove to the store. We bought all the food. Then we made the pie. It was yummy!

Prewrite for draft of "Making a Pie"

Then reveal the 9-grid format for the prewrite. Discuss the differences between it and the BME prewrite (e.g., more boxes so the writer can prewrite more details and thus write a longer draft). By creating more "frames" within the graphic organizer, students naturally expand their thinking and their details. Expanded details in the prewrite lead to a more developed "middle" in the first draft.

Point out the combination of written details (no sentences) and quick sketches that create a storyboard effect. The words and visuals help students produce a well-developed piece. This prewrite will become a powerful tool in writing a strong, meaty first draft. Finally, read aloud the writing sample that corresponds to the 9-grid storyboard.

9-grid storyboard for "Making a Pie"

MAKING A PIE

I was going to help my mom make a pie for Thanksgiving. After we made a list of the ingredients we needed, we drove to the store.

I pushed the cart up and down the aisles. Sometimes my mom let me pick the items off the shelf. When we had all the important food, we went to pay. My mom gave the worker the money, and he said thank you.

When we got home, we read the recipe card. We mixed all the ingredients. I poured the batter, while my mom perfected the crust. Then we put the pie in the oven. We ate it for dessert on Thanksgiving. It was yummy!

New draft of "Making a Pie" based on 9-grid storyboard

INDEPENDENT STUDENT WRITING ACTIVITY

Provide students with a writing topic to prewrite using the 9-grid storyboard (see page 36). Remind them to utilize a combination of word details and quick sketches. When students have finished, consider the following options:

Option 1: For added experience with the 9-grid storyboard, give them a second topic to prewrite.

Option 2: Have them utilize their prewrite to begin writing a first draft.

GROUP SHARE

Have students bring their storyboards to Group Share to reveal the different ways they developed and planned the assigned topic.

LESSON EXTENSION Using the top-left box as the beginning, and the bottom-right box as the ending, have students plan a beginning and ending that are tied together, as taught in Lesson 6 on pages 29–32.

NOTE If moving from three planning boxes to nine is overwhelming for your students, consider having them first simply develop the middle portion in three sections.

Adaptation of 3-grid storyboard.

LESSON 7: DEVELOP THE MIDDLE

Name _____ Date _____

9-Grid Storyboard

Trait-Based Writing: Lessons and Activities © 2009 by Kristina Smekens, Scholastic Teaching Resources

Transition Sentences

Initially, most young writers transition between ideas using words and phrases like *and*, *and then* or *so then*. This typically prompts a teacher to begin instruction on time order words—*first, second, next, then*, and *finally*.

As students further develop ideas into paragraphs, they need to be aware of how to make fluid transitions from one subtopic to the next. Simply dropping in a transition word like *next, although* or *however* will not achieve the smoothest connection of ideas. It's necessary to introduce students to the concept of transition sentences.

Illustrate the function of a smooth transition by comparing it to the blended colors of variegated yarn. The blue turns blue-purple and then solid purple. This is what a transition sentence should do, too. Its purpose is to move the reader gently from paragraph A to paragraph B, connecting the ideas as they read.

Mini-Lesson

Paragraphs should be connected by transitions. The purpose of a transition is to alert the reader of a shift between ideas or subtopics. The smoothest, most fluid transitions connect the previous paragraph to the next one in a single *sentence*.

The following examples show two paragraphs from a descriptive piece. The writer is describing her kitchen in Paragraph A and her living room in Paragraph B.

Paragraph A

My kitchen is not very trendy. It is filled with wicker baskets, pink and blue wooden hearts, and the wallpaper is outdated.

Paragraph B

Technology and electronic gadgets are scattered throughout my living room. There is a huge flat-screen TV mounted on the wall. The leather furniture is arranged so no matter where you sit, the surround sound is perfect.

If you consider that the paragraphs are colored, like variegated yarn, then consider Paragraph A (about the kitchen) as the blue text and Paragraph B (about the living room) as the purple text. A transition sentence needs to be added to reference what is mentioned in Paragraph A and to introduce what the reader will learn in Paragraph B. This needs to be a blue-purple sentence transition.

NOTE Besides color, another way to display the shift from Paragraph A to Paragraph B is to utilize a different typestyle. For example, Paragraph A might be underlined and Paragraph B might be italicized.

Paragraph A

My kitchen is not very trendy. It is filled with wicker baskets, pink and blue wooden hearts, and the wallpaper is outdated.

Paragraph B

Technology and electronic gadgets are scattered throughout my living room. There is a huge flat-screen TV mounted on the wall. The leather furniture is arranged so no matter where you sit, the surround sound is perfect.

Reveal one or two of the transition-sentence examples below.

My kitchen may be old-fashioned, but my living room is high tech.

My friends would rather not hang out in the kitchen; they like the living room better.

You'll find baskets in the kitchen and technology in the living room.

Have students brainstorm other possible transition sentences. Be sure they don't assume there is only one correct transition sentence. The key is simply to connect the two different ideas; there are multiple ways to do that.

Continue to practice drafting transition sentences orally: Create your own Paragraph A and Paragraph B information, and then challenge students to link them with a single sentence (see suggestions on page 39–40). There is no sense moving this skill into written form until it is something students can achieve orally.

Paragraph A

I love our classroom. It has colorful book baskets and beanbags in the reading nook. There are chicks chirping in the incubator. The bulletin boards are filled with all our wonderful writings.

Transition Sentence: _____

Paragraph B

The school playground has three sizes of slides, a tunnel and a climbing wall. Most kids spend their time on the trampoline that the PTO just bought us. There are lots of squeals and screams as kids enjoy recess.

Paragraph A

The house was decorated for the big surprise party. With the lights turned off, no one could see the helium balloons, the crepe paper, or the dozens of people hiding behind furniture.

Transition Sentence: _____

Paragraph B

Mr. and Mrs. Smith and their daughter, the birthday girl, walked into the house. With one big "SURPRISE!" the party began.

Paragraph A

Taking care of a pet is a big responsibility. Every day the owner must feed him, water him, clean up after him, and more. There are always chores to be done.

Transition Sentence: _____

Paragraph B

Animals are loveable. They provide great companionship for humans. They listen when no one else will. They really are "man's best friend."

Paragraph A

Rushing around in the morning, kids all over are getting ready for school. Putting on clothes, finishing hygiene routines, loading up their backpacks, and chowing down breakfast are typical tasks in the morning.

Transition Sentence: _____

Paragraph B

Friends hang out and chat at the bus stop. When the bus comes, they all load up, sitting in the same seats, with the same classmates, every day.

INDEPENDENT STUDENT WRITING ACTIVITY

Move beyond creating oral transitions to writing transition sentences. Have students take a current draft and cut apart the paragraphs. Give them strips of colored paper and have them reassemble the writing, taping a colored strip between each paragraph. Challenge students to write transition sentences on the colored strips connecting the different paragraphs.

[left] Cut apart the paragraphs.
[right] Attach colored strips with transition sentences.

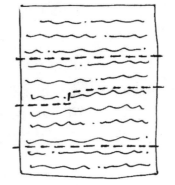
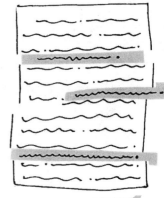

GROUP SHARE

Have students share some of their revised transition sentences. See if the class can guess the topic of the paragraphs before and after the transition sentence. A well-written transition references both ideas.

LESSON EXTENSION

If the ideas in students' writing aren't developed enough, it may be difficult to break apart the paragraphs and write whole transition sentences. An option is to provide students with excerpt paragraphs from literature and have them draft sample transition sentences between each set of paragraphs. Then, reveal the actual transition sentence.

TRAIT-BASED WRITING

Hearing Voice

LESSON RATIONALE	Voice can be described as the writer's attitude toward the topic. Once students can "hear" and identify the type of voice within literature, then it will be easier for them to attempt it within their own writing.

LESSON TRIGGER	Thinking of voice in terms of attitude or emotion easily triggers the image of changing facial expressions: *furious, sad, overjoyed, frightened, love struck, nervous,* and so on.

Mini-Lesson

If the trait of voice is characterized as the writer's attitude toward the topic (or character's attitude about a situation), first read Saxton Freymann's *How Are You Peeling? Food With Moods* (Scholastic, 1999). The fruits and vegetables are a perfect first exposure to voice. If you don't have access to Freymann's book, another option would be to collect multiple photos from magazines, out-of-date calendars, greeting cards, and so on. Look for images that depict people in a variety of emotional and physical states and facial expressions that show a lot of exaggerated feeling. Have students name the emotional state or attitude of each "character" in the picture book or collected images. Consider starting a class list of types of voices. Then read aloud and discuss the two writing samples.

Dear Shadow,
Oh! I long to see your beatiful wings again. I miss you so much! Yes, I remember when I first got you as a small, black, squirmy fellow. Then the next stage and the next. When I saw you as a butterfly I was so happy! But when I figured out I had to let you go. I was heartbroken. I hope you are safe. Be careful. Be hopeful. Keep going.

Love from,
Terese

MY WORST DAY EVER

My worst day ever is when my Grandpa Bob died. It was heartbreaking to me. I cried for weeks and weeks until my dad and mom told me he wants to be happy and he's in a better place now. We watched videos of Grandpa Bob. He had a great life with a great family. He always called me Michelle because he had cancer and couldn't remember as well.

We picked a flower to keep forever and ever. I still have it. And the family was there praying, while we watched them bury him on the coldest day, where nobody could see the sun. While the preacher was preaching, the sun popped out. The preacher said it was Grandpa Bob saying why are you down, you should be up. Everyone just cried, until I knew he was all right. I smiled and Daddy pushed me up to the front to see everyone, and to say some stuff to let it out. So I did. I got a big reward, but nothing to hold or to spend or to play with. I got hugs and kisses from the family. And that's all I really needed after all was love and to know he's in a better place.

First, have students attempt to identify *how* the writer feels about Shadow (page 41). Challenge them to identify the emotions or attitudes they hear in the letter (e.g., sincere, loving, disappointed, worried, hopeful, encouraging, and so on).

Then, have students attempt to identify *how* the writer feels about the death and funeral of her grandpa. Challenge them to identify the emotion or attitude they hear in the piece (e.g., sadness, loneliness, reminiscence, sincerity, loving, hopeful, bittersweet, nervous, loved, appreciative, and so on.).

There may not be just one attitude in each piece of writing. Discuss that at different points in the piece the reader may hear different emotions. That's not unusual. Sometimes a piece has a consistent tone or voice, but often a reader hears many emotions. This may have a lot to do with the reader's own background knowledge and personal experiences. The important skill to target is simply the fact that students hear any attitude, or voice, at all.

INDEPENDENT STUDENT WRITING ACTIVITY

List several topics and corresponding attitudes as shown below. Have students jot a quick write for each topic to utilize the indicated attitude.

TOPIC	VOICE
Being chased by a large, angry dog	fearful
Floating on a raft in a pool/lake	lazy, relaxed
Taking a timed test	nervous, rushed
Getting a doctor's shot	scared, painful

GROUP SHARE

Have several students share one of their quick writes from the Independent Student Writing Activity.

LESSON EXTENSION

Before beginning their next pieces, have students note how they *feel* about the topic written at the top of their papers. Focusing on their intended attitudes while drafting helps writers convey those ideas with specific word choice.

Finding Voice

LESSON RATIONALE	As students begin recognizing and identifying voice, take them to the next level by having them identify the specific words and phrases that elicit the attitude.
LESSON TRIGGER	Continue utilizing the concept of conveying moods and attitudes through facial expressions.

Mini-Lesson

Read aloud the writing sample below.

> I'd Rather (ANYTHING HERE) Than Have Music
> Have you ever had something you would rather do than something you don't like? Well I do.
> I would rather mow all of Asia than have music class. I would even mow every teeny, tiny little bit of grass on the continent.
> I would go without eating my favorite food, which is chicken and noodles. I'd suffer rather than have music.
> I would rather get punched in the stomach by a football player that is really really strong than have music.
> There are lot of other things I would rather do than have music. I really don't like music because we have to play recorders.

Discuss the voice or feelings the students "hear" in the writer's attitude toward music class (e.g., sarcastic, complaining, annoyed, and so on). Then, take it to the next level. Ask students to identify which words or phrases elicit the voice(s) they identified. Challenge them to find and mark (underline or highlight) the specific words and phrases that contain the sarcastic/complaining/annoyed voice. If students can "find" voice, they are closer to being able to write with a strong voice. Here are some sample responses.

Well I do. (sarcastic)

even mow every teeny, tiny little bit of grass (sarcastic)

suffer (shows severity of dislike)

rather get punched in the stomach (shows severity of dislike)

because we have to play recorders (complaining)

After studying voice within an entire piece, spend time dissecting it within small passages. Using the excerpts below, show students voice-less sentences, and voice-filled revisions. Demonstrate how a simple sentence or idea can be transformed into a voice-rich passage. Discuss the originals versus the revisions. Identify the words that contribute to the strong voice.

 NOTE You may prefer to utilize picture books or excerpts from literature instead of the student writing samples/excerpts provided here.

Voice-less Sentence 1:

Good luck, Shadow the butterfly.

Revision including a "hopeful" voice:

When I figured out I had to let you go, Shadow, I was heartbroken. I hope you are safe. Be careful. Be hopeful. Keep going.

Voice-less Sentence 2:

I'm good at sneaking up on people.

Revision including a "confident" voice:

You couldn't hear me even if I was wearing nylon pants on a creaky stairway. I could sneak up on you in a fully lighted room without objects to hide behind. I am a master of the stealth technique.

Voice-less Sentence 3:

I hated sitting through the piano recital. It took forever!

Revision including a "bored and disgusted" voice:

The kid after me played an easy song on the piano. "Easy," I said under my breath. I had a thousand more people to listen to. I sighed. I wished I didn't have to wait much longer.

INDEPENDENT STUDENT WRITING ACTIVITY

Give pairs opportunities to play with this skill by revising the following voice-less sentences to make them voice-rich:

Revise to include a "cherished and adored" voice:

I love the baseball bat my grandpa gave me. It's my favorite present ever.

Revise to include a "frustrated" voice:

For the millionth time, I told my brother to leave me alone.

Revise to include a "nervous" voice:

It was my turn to give my oral book report. I was so nervous walking to the front of the class.

GROUP SHARE

Ask students to share some of their voice-rich sentences and discuss how they transformed the sentences.

LESSON EXTENSION

Have students work with a previous piece of writing or begin a new piece to identify what voice or attitude they want to convey. Then, they should begin writing/revising the piece to achieve that voice. When they have completed this activity, students should read their writing aloud to a partner and discuss the following questions together:

What voice did the listener hear?

What voice was the writer attempting?

What were the strongest, voice-filled words and phrases?

Where was voice weakest?

Armed with new inspiration, students can dive into the revision process.

"Test Lady" Audience

The on-demand writing that a test prompt requires can easily zap a writer's voice. Add to that the stress of a "testing" situation, and many students lose sight of the fact that a real person will actually read their work. Increase your students' motivation and "voice" levels by inventing a "Test Lady" audience for them.

LESSON TRIGGER

Humanize the test-writing genre by giving students a sense of audience for writing prompts. This might include drawing portraits of the Test Lady, dressing up a mannequin, or having someone dress up and be a "guest speaker" for your class.

Mini-Lesson

Many students believe that machines score their statewide, on-demand writing assessments. How would they know that real people will read their work, unless you tell them? So it's time to introduce them to the "Test Lady."

Create a story about having several phone conversations with this test grader. Tell students you don't know what she looks like because you've never met her. You don't even know her name. Explain that this is the lady who reads their responses to writing prompts and scores them. Tell students that she is waiting at the state capitol for the box of writing from your school and that she scores all of the state writings. She gets excited about specific details, powerful verbs, attention-grabbing hooks, long and meaty middles, and so on.

As you share snippets from these invented conversations, let students know that they will soon be writing for the state assessment, and they will be writing to the Test Lady. Give them the notion that there is a human being at the other end of the writing. Give them a sense of audience, because with an audience comes a writer's voice.

INDEPENDENT STUDENT WRITING ACTIVITY

Consider giving students time to draw their version of the Test Lady. Having a concrete image of their audience helps them dive into this test-writing genre. Use the reproducible on page 49.

Student's portrait of the "Test Lady"

GROUP SHARE

Ask students to reveal their portraits. Then, hang them at the front of the classroom. This will be a visual reminder to students during the assessment to write to the Test Lady—to write with a sense of who their audience is.

LESSON EXTENSION

Extend this lesson by having students not only consider what the Test Lady looks like, but also the key writing skills they want to remember going into the state assessment.

This student wants to remember to make her stories longer, add similes and metaphors, and add more details and big words.

TRAIT-BASED WRITING

Name _____ Date _____

Self-Assessment

When I am writing to the Test Lady, I will remember to:

1. _____

2. _____

3. _____

4. _____

In my mind, the Test Lady looks like this:

Purple Words

Many teachers have a special name for strong word choice—WOW! Words, Pizzazz Words, Money Words, Sparkle Words, and so on. It's a great idea to recognize specific word choice. But it is even more important that a teacher finds a visual strategy for acknowledging when students use strong words in their writing. Without teacher recognition, students will quickly lose interest in working on intentional word choice.

Alert students to your procedure for celebrating WOW! Words in their writing. A quick stroke of a purple highlighter (or another exotic color) says it all!

Mini-Lesson

To encourage your students to continue playing with word choice and striving for exact language, introduce them to the purple highlighter. Pink, yellow, green, blue, and orange highlighters are pretty common, but the purple highlighter isn't so easy to find. You might have to buy a set of 30 multicolored markers to get a single purple highlighter. Consequently, these markers are rare.

This rarity provides a good comparison to writing. When students use a rare word (rather than settling for a common and predictable one), they will be rewarded with a stroke of purple. It's your way of signaling that they nailed their word choice, and that you noticed.

NOTE This strategy is very efficient for the busy classroom teacher, too. Highlighting excellent word choice is faster than noting "Great word choice!" or "Vivid Vocabulary!" on student writing. And students like the look of all that purple on their writing!

Make a transparency of "Stealth" on page 51. Display it and use a purple marker to indicate the words and phrases students thought were strong.

STEALTH

You couldn't hear me if I was wearing nylon pants on a creaky stairway. I could sneak up on you in a fully-lighted room with no objects to hide behind. I am a master of the stealth technique. I have the ability and skill to make myself seem weightless and invisible. But not literally of course. My name is Andrew Smith, (wannabe S.W.A.T., covert operative, and special forces officer).

I first noticed this skill when I was about six, and I loved to sneak up on people. I would speed silently up and down stairs, and after a while I'd get responses like "I didn't know you were here," or "How did you . . . you were just downstairs . . . huh?" After that, I noticed that I could take advantage of this skill and use it to get a midnight snack, or run away covertly when my mom was about to ask me to clean my room.

If you too want to have this specialty, then listen up. We will start with the skill to be silent. Here is an example. Let's say you are trying to scare your brother and there are creaky stairs that you have to cross. It requires knowledge of where to step. You should plant your foot on the very edge of each step, that will be the least likely spot to make noise. If you are light enough, you could jump from step to step landing silently on the corners, (this would also increase speed). So remember, it is the knowledge of where to step that will help most.

Next let's talk about being unseen. It is the asset of all objects that are good for hiding behind. Use all the objects as tools, while you use your skill to step quietly. This is the way to practice, but once you're good enough, you could step up to someone unnoticed without objects to hide behind.

That is a way to be covert.

LESSON 12: PURPLE WORDS

After marking the "purple words" in this piece, discuss why students like these words so much. Brainstorm examples of less powerful synonyms for some of the strong words (e.g., *can/have the ability, go/speed silently, say things/responses, to be good at something/specialty*).

NOTE **Point out that some of their favorites are phrases and not just individual words (e.g., *master of stealth technique; skill to be silent*). Sometimes strengthening word choice requires students to rework whole sentences and not just substitute words. Highlighting two or three consecutive words will indicate to students that they used a powerful purple phrase.**

After identifying examples of great word choice, work as a class to write a definition. What qualifies a word or phrase for stroking from the purple high-lighter? Qualifications might include ideas like the following: not the typical word everyone else might use; an exact word, not a general word; a big word sounded out and stretched out.

INDEPENDENT STUDENT WRITING ACTIVITY

Have students select a previous piece of writing from their writing folders and identify a couple of dinky words (also known as "R.I.P. words," "Dead words," "Tired words," "Buried words," and so on) in the writing. Challenge them to replace the dinky words with purple-worthy words or phrases.

GROUP SHARE

Ask students to share some of their original and revised words/phrases.

LESSON EXTENSION Maintain a list of powerful words. Whether it's a class list on chart paper or individual lists in students' writers' notebook, designate a place to begin logging these "purple" words. Add to it regularly. Look for strong word choice within your daily read-alouds and compile them under the title "Great Words We Noticed in Our Reading." These lists will become a great resource for students during writing time.

Shades of Words

LESSON RATIONALE

Somewhere along the line, many students begin to misunderstand the purpose of a thesaurus. They come to believe it contains a list of words that all mean exactly the same thing. And that's when they become "thesaurus pickers." When revising for better word choice, they take out a word, and put in a word, . . . take out a word, and put in a word. Eventually, their pieces make little sense.

This lesson shows writers that although a group of synonyms may have some commonalities, each word has its own specific meaning. Strong writers are choosy when it comes to selecting just the right word to send just the right message.

LESSON TRIGGER

Utilize an 8-color and 64-color box of crayons to point out how the "shades" of words increase with the bigger quantity. A box of 64 crayons with multiple shades of the same color works well to demonstrate how synonyms are "shades" of a general word.

NOTE Before executing this lesson, presort the 64-color box of crayons so that all the blues are together, all the reds are together, and so on.

Mini-Lesson

Holding up the 8-color box of crayons and the 64-color box of crayons, ask students to tell you what is different about the two boxes, besides that the 64-color box has "more." Press them to tell you what it has more of? (You want students to recognize that it has more "shades" of the same 8 colors. There are still blues, greens, reds, oranges, yellows, and so on, but within the 64-color box set, there are more shades of each color.)

Compare the idea of shades of color to shades of words—also known as synonyms. For example, *blue* is a general word, and it has synonyms like *peacock*, *periwinkle*, *indigo*, and so on. (Each of these synonyms can be found on the side of a crayon.)

Move the lesson from color adjectives to other general adjectives like *big*.

Have students identify shades of *big*—*large, giant, enormous, huge,* and so on. Clarify that they are not creating an opposites list; it is not a list of words ranging from *big* to *small.* Rather this list will range from least-*big* to most-*big.* Compare it to the activity with the crayons: It's like putting all the blue crayons in order from lightest *blue* to darkest *blue.*

Use the graphic organizers on pages 56 and 57 to list the color adjectives and general adjectives.

Better words for _____pink_____

☐ cotton candy _____

☐ carnation _____

☐ magenta _____

☐ mulberry _____

☐ _____

☐ _____

☐ _____

Better words for _____big_____

huge _____

large _____

enourmous _____

ginormous _____

giant _____

gigantic _____

_____ _____

_____ _____

_____ _____

_____ _____

INDEPENDENT STUDENT WRITING ACTIVITY

Pair students and assign an overused word to each set of partners: *fun, mad, hot, cold, nice, happy, mean, small, ugly,* and so on. Have them brainstorm as many "shades" of that word as they can think of on their own. Once partners have exhausted their thinking, have them swap lists with another pair. See if they can add more "shades" to each other's lists. Encourage pairs to think of synonym word phrases, too (e.g., *mad* could include *red hot*). To wrap up the activity, you might suggest students utilize a thesaurus for additional inspiration.

GROUP SHARE

Allow time for each pair to share its favorite words from the lists. You might end this sharing time by declaring all the "general" words at the top of each list (e.g., *blue, big,* and so on) as "dead words" that students can no longer use in their writing.

Build a kid-friendly classroom thesaurus with students' lists. Collect the synonym lists in a single folder. Add several blank template pages, so students can add more synonym word lists over time.

LESSON EXTENSION

Be prepared: Most students will begin utilizing better words in their writing, but they still may not be making the precise word choice you were hoping for. Return to the crayon analogy in a follow-up lesson. Compare students' word choice to a 24-color box of crayons. Let them know that you've noticed their efforts to use better words. For example, you notice they aren't using *mad* (an 8-color box crayon word). Rather, they have chosen *angry*. It's a better word; it's a 24-color box crayon word. However, *furious, disappointed, frustrated,* would all be more precise, and thus earn the title of a 64-color box crayon word. Encourage students to keep digging for just the right words.

Name _____ Date _____

Better words for _____

Trait-Based Writing: Lessons and Activities © 2009 by Kristina Smekens, Scholastic Teaching Resources

Name _____ Date _____

Better words for _____

_____   _____

_____   _____

_____   _____

_____   _____

_____   _____

_____   _____

_____   _____

Taboo Words

| LESSON **RATIONALE** | Sometimes students need a gentle nudge to experiment with language. Old writing habits are hard to break. This lesson helps pull students out of their "word rut" by identifying a set of words that are temporarily off-limits, or taboo. |

| LESSON **TRIGGER** | The forbidden or banned symbol makes a great visual when listing taboo words. |

Mini-Lesson

When working on developing the trait of word choice in your writers, don't just focus on revising for strong word choice. Teach them that powerful word choice can be achieved by avoiding the predictable words and phrases associated with a topic.

For example, when writing about winter, a simple and predictable description might read like the following:

WINTER

It's snowing big white flakes. It's cold. I'm freezing. I can see my breath.

To avoid this problem, have students name five common words and phrases associated with winter. Ask: "What are the first five words people think of when they think about winter?" List their responses on the board. As the sample above suggests, the list might include *snow, cold, white, flakes, freezing,* and so on.

Label the words on the list "taboo" for the topic of winter. Explain that *taboo* means these words are now off limits in students' writing. It will force students to stretch their word choice and utilize less predictable language.

TRAIT-BASED WRITING

NOTE These words are different than "dead" or "banished" words. Taboo words are only prohibited for a particular topic. It's not that *freezing* is a weak word; it's just too predictable for the topic of winter. And for that reason, you want to temporarily make that word taboo.

When pushed to be more selective in his word choice by avoiding taboo words, this writer's second draft is much more descriptive.

OUTSIDE IN THE WINTER

My fingers and toes are numb. My red-face is stiff. Every time I breathe in through my drippy nose, I feel miniature icicles forming in my nostrils.

INDEPENDENT STUDENT WRITING ACTIVITY

Give students time to practice thinking and stretching beyond their ordinary vocabulary. Have them select a topic from the following possibilities:

Favorite food	Birthday party
Messy bedroom	Lost and scared
Snowstorm	Getting hurt
Environmental pollution	Healthy eating
Embarrassing moment	Bike riding
Mother's Day	Vacation

Based on the topic, each student should generate a taboo word list. Then tell them to write on the topic, avoiding the predetermined taboo words. Don't necessarily look for students to write an entire piece. Just give them some time to experiment with language and dabble with the topic in a few sentences.

NOTE To differentiate this lesson for struggling writers, suggest they list 1–5 taboo words. Encourage stronger writers to list 6–10 taboo words.

GROUP SHARE

Ask volunteers to share excerpts of their writing. Allow time for class discussion. Prompt discussion with the following questions: "How difficult was it to avoid the taboo words? How did you come up with alternative words? How does this sort of activity help you become more creative in your word choices?"

LESSON EXTENSION

Announce a new writing procedure similar to prewriting: Before students begin their first drafts, they must think about not only the details to include (prewrite), but also the general words they want to avoid (taboo words). At the top of their writing, students should identify 3–10 predictable words to avoid. They routinely make their own taboo list before each writing.

Dead Verbs

LESSON RATIONALE

Verbs are the engine of a sentence. They are the power words that drive the sentence. Students need some guidance not only in developing stronger verb choice, but also in knowing which overused verbs to delete from their writer's vocabulary.

LESSON TRIGGER

An R.I.P. paper tombstone posted on the classroom wall is a great way display a list of "dead" or "buried verbs."

R.I.P. poster for "dead verbs"

NOTE It might be easier to identify overused verbs if you maintain a list based on students' writings. For several weeks, note the verbs they utilize repeatedly within their writing. Identify these as the first verbs to bury.

Mini-Lesson

Explain to students that their writing has been plagued with overused and weak verb choices. (Their overused "favorites" will probably include *go/went, get/got, like/love, do/did, make/made, take/took, says/said, putting/put,* and a series of linking and helping verbs. Any one of these verbs in small doses is tolerable, but unfortunately, students tend to rely on them.) Point out that these words are also too general in meaning. Write the following example on the board: I <u>took</u> the dollar off her desk.

Emphasize that good writers aim to be precise in their descriptions so their writing is clear for their readers. The verb *took* in the example is too general. Depending on which verb is substituted, the meaning of this sentence can change. Write the following examples on the board and discuss them:

I <u>borrowed</u> the dollar from her desk. (implies the taker had permission)

I <u>snatched</u> the dollar from her desk. (implies a fast and aggressive grab)

I <u>sneaked</u> the dollar from her desk. (implies a theft)

Make a very specific list of "dead verbs" and post the list in the classroom.

Now that the dead verbs have been identified and buried, it's time to focus on verb alternatives. This will require broadening students' oral and written vocabularies. Use the sentence-story below to have students brainstorm verb replacements for the *get/got* verbs that fit the context of the original sentences. Sample replacements appear in parentheses.

NOTE You can more literally "bury" and banish specific overused verbs. This could include a ceremonial "funeral" of sorts by writing the weak verbs on helium balloons and releasing them *forever!*

"GET" OUT OF HERE

He got up at seven. (woke, hopped, jumped)

He got his own breakfast. (made, prepared, cooked)

He got cereal on his shirt. (spilled, dribbled, dropped)

He got a towel from the sink. (grabbed, fetched, used)

Then, he got his backpack. (found, organized, snatched)

He hurried to get done with his homework. (finish, complete)

He got his coat and got to school just in time. (grabbed, found, retrieved/arrived, hurried, rushed)

For additional practice, have students revise the verb choices in the next two sentence-stories. Suggestions are provided in parentheses.

PUT "PUT" AWAY

My mom put me in charge of cleaning my room. (ordered, delegated)

I put the clean clothes back onto hangers. (returned, rehung)

I put my dirty dishes to the kitchen. (returned, carried, carted)

As I put away my toys, I saw one was broken. (sorted, organized)

I put it in the trash. (discarded, tossed, pitched)

I put away all my sister's hair accessories. (gathered up, scooped up, sorted)

I put all the school papers in a folder (slid, tucked), and put that folder in my backpack. (returned, slid, tucked)

Then I put my hands on my hips and smiled at my clean room. (rested, placed)

62

"MAKE" A BETTER VERB CHOICE

My mom told me to <u>make</u> lunch for the family. (<u>prepare, cook, bake</u>)

I <u>made</u> ham and cheese sandwiches. (<u>crafted, decided on, selected, chose</u>)

I <u>made</u> them with frilly toothpicks. (<u>decorated, accessorized</u>)

Also, I <u>made</u> them into shapes. (<u>cut, carved, arranged</u>)

I thought I needed to <u>make</u> about 10 sandwiches. (<u>prepare, assemble</u>)

But I was having so much fun, I <u>made</u> too many! (<u>completed, prepared</u>)

NOTE To increase the challenge, announce that students can't repeat any verbs within the same sentence-story.

INDEPENDENT STUDENT WRITING ACTIVITY

Encourage students to select two recent pieces of writing and mark every "dead verb." They should then revise for more specific verb choice.

GROUP SHARE

Have students reveal their original and revised sentences.

LESSON EXTENSION

Follow up this initial mini-lesson with instruction on how to reconstruct a sentence to include a better verb. It is often not as simple as replacing or substituting a "dead verb" for a more precise one. The entire sentence structure may need to be rearranged: *I <u>put</u> the clean clothes back onto hangers . . . I <u>rehung</u> the clean clothes that I'd thrown on the floor.*

Another lesson extension might include challenging students to write their own mini sentence-story for any of these combinations: *take/took, did/do, like/love, go/went.* Then, the class can work together on revising them.

Hearing Punctuation

L E S S O N RATIONALE

There is a close connection between smooth sentence fluency and the trait of conventions. A writer's use of punctuation marks (or lack of use) can either help or hinder a reader's fluency. However, for some students, simply memorizing punctuation rules isn't helpful. This lesson teaches them to listen and pay attention to how their voice changes when they read different texts with different punctuation marks.

L E S S O N TRIGGER

Students need to "hear" punctuation marks. The whisper phone (also known as a fluency phone) makes a great trigger to remind them that this is an auditory trait. You hear fluency; you don't read it.

Mini-Lesson

Build a chart with students showing the punctuation marks they are already familiar with, as shown at the right. Emphasize what happens to the reader's voice when it "hits" each mark.

Give students the opportunity to focus on reading punctuation marks and hearing their voices change. Use the alphabet passages on page 65 to have students do a choral read. As you read along, be sure students' voices are adjusting for each punctuation mark at the end of the "sentences."

Punctuation and Voice chart

TRAIT-BASED WRITING

NOTE Reading the alphabet (rather than a passage of literature) reduces students' concentration on decoding and phonics. It puts students' attention on manipulating their voices based on the varying punctuation marks. You could achieve the same goal using consecutive numbers, or math facts, as shown.

AB?	A and BC.	1, 2, and 3.	3!
CDEF.	D?	4?	6, 9, and 12.
GH!	EF, GH, and I.	5 . . . 6, 7.	15?
I?	JK!	8!	18 and 21.
J.	LM . . . N.	9, 10, 11.	24! 27!
KL.	OP.	12?	30.
MN?	QRS?	13 and 14.	33 . . . 36, 39?
OPQ!	T!	15, 16, and 17.	
RS!	UV; WX.	18!	
TUV?	YZ?	19?	
WX.		20.	
YZ!			

Alphabet passages for choral reading.   *Number passages for choral reading.*

Ultimately, students should "see" the punctuation mark coming. That said, be sure they also practice reading punctuation marks when the sentences are side by side, and not just stacked on top of one another. This is referred to as text wrapping.

> A and BC. D? EF, GH and
>
> I. JK! LM . . . N. OP. QRS? T! UV;
>
> WX. YZ?

Alphabet passage that is text wrapped.

Obviously, the ultimate purpose of this lesson isn't that students can read the alphabet, but rather that they can read punctuation marks accurately within context. Therefore, conclude the lesson by having them choral read a passage that includes multiple punctuation marks. A favorite is *Yo! Yes?* by Chris Raschka, (Scholastic, 1994). This picture book uses few words, so struggling readers can focus on the punctuation and not get bogged down decoding the phonics. Let the students practice reading and manipulating their voices depending on the punctuation mark.

INDEPENDENT STUDENT WRITING ACTIVITY

Have students work in pairs to develop their own "sentences" utilizing the alphabet or numbers. Encourage them to include a variety of punctuation marks. If students write directly onto transparency film, then the class can choral read them aloud.

GROUP SHARE

Ask students to reveal their writing on overhead transparencies and encourage the class to read the samples aloud. Review how their voices were affected by the different punctuation marks.

LESSON EXTENSION

Draw the connection between this lesson and students' self-editing their own writing. Encourage them to reread their writing aloud, listening for changes in their voice. When they hear their own voice pause, stop, or say a word loudly, then they should check that they utilized the correct punctuation mark. This alerts readers as to how to adjust their voices, too.

Slinky Sentences

<table>
<tr>
<td>

**L E S S O N
RATIONALE**

</td>
<td>

Students tend to repeat a simple sentence pattern over and over.

</td>
</tr>
</table>

I went home. I got a snack. I watched TV.

Not only do the sentences usually begin the same way, but they also tend to be the same length. Whether the pattern is short and choppy or long and gangly, fluency isn't achieved if the sentence lengths are not varied.

<table>
<tr>
<td>

**L E S S O N
T R I G G E R**

</td>
<td>

To illustrate varied sentence lengths, look for a toy or an object that stretches, like a Slinky®.

</td>
</tr>
</table>

Mini-Lesson

Illustrate the concept of varying sentence length by using a Slinky. Stretch it to represent a long sentence (more than 10 words). Compress the toy to represent a short sentence (1–5 words). Slightly elongate it for a medium-length sentence (6–10 words). Explain to students that a single piece of writing should include sentences of different lengths. If it does, then it passes the "Slinky Test."

NOTE **Find strong, Slinky-Test-passing excerpts from literature. Reveal them to students. Stretch the Slinky or other toy after reading aloud each sentence to show students how it is moving throughout the passage.**

Reveal the original "Winter Tunnels" piece on page 68. Without telling students this sample is weak, have them attempt to adjust the Slinky after every sentence. Inevitably, someone will announce, "This one's boring. All the sentences are practically the same length." Mission accomplished! That's the point to make with this weak sample: It's no fun to hold a Slinky you can't move, and it's no fun to read a piece with sentences that are all the same length. It is boring!

> ### WINTER TUNNELS
>
> My brother and I were making snow tunnels. My brother's tunnel got broken. He thought I broke it. That's when it started. He ambushed me with snowballs. They flew through the air like jets. I slid in my tunnel. I got hit and got angry. I crawled out and threw ice at him. He caught the ice and threw it back. Snow was dripping down my shirt. Eventually I lost and went back inside.

Dissect the individual sentences in "Winter Tunnels," noting how many words are in each sentence. Guide students to recognize that this

NOTE If you don't have access to multiple Slinkys, consider having the students use their arm-spans to represent the length of each sentence.

piece doesn't pass the Slinky Test because all the sentences are the same length. Then, have them work to revise the sentences by orally lengthening or shortening one or two of them.

Reveal the author's actual revision of "Winter Tunnels" shown below. Have students utilize their Slinkys again (or their arms) after every sentence. Does the revision pass the test?

> ### WINTER TUNNELS
>
> My brother and I were making tunnels in a snow mound. My brother's tunnel broke. He stared at me, thinking I broke it. That's when it started. He ambushed me with snowballs. They flew through the air like jets. AAHHH! I ran, dove, and slid into my tunnel to stay away from him. I got hit. I got angry. I crawled out of the tunnel and started throwing giant pieces of ice back at him. He fired back. Snow and ice chips were dripping down my shirt. Eventually I lost and went back inside.

INDEPENDENT STUDENT WRITING ACTIVITY

Ask students to apply the Slinky Test to their own writing. Have them reread and demonstrate the length of each sentence with toys (or using their arm spans). If their sentences need variety, encourage students to add or delete words to make some sentences longer and some shorter.

GROUP SHARE

Review the power of the Slinky Test and how it improves sentence fluency. Ask students to share some of their original and revised sentences. Discuss their strategies for adding or removing words.

LESSON EXTENSION

Follow up this lesson with strategies for lengthening and shortening sentences. Create a chart to display in the classroom.

MAKING SENTENCES LONGER

1. Add a descriptive detail (color, name, kind, and so on).

   original: The cat was playful.

   revised: The charcoal gray cat was cute and playful.

2. Add a comparison detail (smell, taste, touch, sound, sight).

   original: His bedroom was messy.

   revised: His messy bedroom stunk like the boys' locker room.

3. Add a phrase about how the character said something.

   original: "Get out!" she screamed.

   revised: "Get out!" she screamed, with her hands on her hips.

4. Add a phrase that explains something or gives examples.

   original: Plants need nutrients.

   revised: Plants need nutrients, like water and fertilizer, to grow.

MAKING SENTENCES SHORTER

1. Take out any "and" or "and then" phrases, and separate the sentences.

    original: I put on my snowsuit and my boots and went outside and played in the snow.

    revised: I put on my snowsuit and my boots. I went outside and played in the snow.

2. If you have several adjectives in a row, substitute them for a single stronger one.

    original: His hair was bright reddish-orange and had gold parts.

    revised: His hair was sunset orange.

3. Take out parts of the sentence that repeat the same thing.

    original: I walked through the cold river and felt the freezing water on my ice-cold feet.

    revised: I walked through the river with ice-cold feet.

Sentence Length for Impact

The words in a sentence convey an idea or message. But the sentence structure, and particularly the sentence length, can convey a tone or underlying meaning.

The previous lesson (Lesson 17: Slinky Sentences, pp. 67–70) focused on varying sentence lengths within a piece of writing. However, good writing is more than just varying long and short sentences. Strong writers intentionally utilize a short sentence for punch and skillfully craft a long sentence to help with pacing. The shifting of "speeds" within the writing dictates how the reader interprets the overall message.

L E S S O N TRIGGER

Using a Slinky, represent the speed of a sentence by compressing it quickly for short sentences and slowly stretching it for long sentences.

Mini-Lesson

Explain that in a narrative story, the sentence length conveys an underlying meaning. Discuss the information in the charts.

> **Several short sentences (1–5 words each) in a row create a fast-paced mood.** A string of short sentences can be hard-hitting. They create a sense of urgency. Facts, information, or details within short sentences stand out. Often, several short sentences are followed by a longer sentence that "wraps up" or reflects on the fast facts.

Original passage:
Janet had to hurry because the bus was coming. She heard the wheels squealing and saw the bus coming down the street. She ran out the door and down the drive to catch only the stench of lingering exhaust fumes.

 Revised passage:
Janet had to hurry. The bus was coming. She heard its wheels squeal. She saw its yellow face. It turned down her street. She had no more time. She ran out the door and down the drive, catching only the stench of lingering exhaust fumes.

Long sentences (10 or more words) create a slower pace of reading.
When you want the reader to linger and think, create a longer sentence. Slow, quiet moments (or when the character is thinking and reflecting) should be written in long sentences. This forces the reader to slow down as he or she wades through the words, pausing to breathe for punctuation marks. But be careful—too many long sentences can bog down a passage.

Original passage:
Tiffany felt lazy. She grabbed a book. She flopped on the couch. She read.

 Revised passage:
Feeling lazy, Tiffany grabbed a book and flopped on the couch to read.

Repeating the same word, phrase or sentence increases the impact.
There is *redundancy*, and then there is *repetition*. Overusing a word/phrase to the point where the reader is annoyed is *redundancy*. *Repetition* is done for impact, to articulate a key point. It builds; it crescendos. Used intentionally, a recurring word, phrase, or sentence gathers the reader's attention with a snowball effect.

Original passage:
As soon as he threw it, Brad knew they were sunk. The baseball pierced the living room window. CRASH! Not a small, perfect hole, but a gaping void.

 Revised passage:
As soon as he threw it, Brad knew they were sunk. The baseball pierced the living room window. CRASH! Not a small, perfect hole, but a gaping void with hunks of glass continuing to fall. CRASH! One by one. CRASH! CRASH! CRASH! Every time another piece fell, their faces winced at the noise.

Next, select a "fast-action" topic and a "calm and slow" topic from the lists on page 73. As a class, draft a couple of sample sentences for each topic. Challenge students to practice manipulating their sentence lengths intentionally.

FAST, ANGRY, URGENT TOPICS

- Late for the bus
- Running a race
- Getting in line for recess
- Responding to a fire alarm/fire drill
- Being frustrated by a sibling
- Being picked on or bullied
- Being chased by an angry dog
- Hurrying to the car in a thunderstorm
- Getting a shot from the doctor
- Taking a timed test
- Playing a fast-action video game

SLOW, CALM, RELAXED TOPICS

- Riding in the car on a long trip
- Watching cookies bake
- Watching a boring event (recital, ball game)
- Floating on a raft in a lake
- Watching snowflakes fall
- Lying on a bed listening to music
- Reading a book
- Painting/coloring a picture
- Blowing bubbles
- Slowly licking an ice-cream cone
- Watching a helium balloon float

INDEPENDENT STUDENT WRITING ACTIVITY

Have students work in pairs/teams to select another "fast" and "slow" topic from the lists and work together to write a paragraph about it. As they write, encourage them to focus on short or long sentence lengths to achieve maximum impact. Remind them also to dabble with word/sentence repetition.

GROUP SHARE

Ask pairs to share their fast-paced and slow-paced paragraphs. Reading drafts aloud will help students determine if the length of their sentences work. Remember, fluency is an auditory trait; you hear it.

LESSON EXTENSION

Teach students that intentional sentence length is also relevant in expository writing.

- Hard-hitting facts and numbers sound better when written in short sentences.

- Reflections, thoughts, and conclusions should be written in long sentences.

- When the writer wants to emphasize an idea or theme, he or she can repeat the word, phrase, or sentence for impact.

LESSON 18: SENTENCE LENGTH FOR IMPACT

Punctuation Walkabout

L E S S O N
RATIONALE

Play off the fact that most writers can learn to "hear" periods (see Lesson 16: Hearing Punctuation, pp. 64–66). They can be taught to listen for sentence endings.

L E S S O N
TRIGGER

Incorporate bodily-kinesthetic movement to represent periods—stomp your feet, clap your hands.

Mini-Lesson

Display one of the writing samples from page 75 that includes the correct use of periods on the overhead. Ask students to pay attention to what happens to your voice when you reach a period. Begin reading aloud, creating a long pause between sentences. Use your finger to track the writing as you read. Be sure to point to periods as you get to them. Students should hear that your voice stops when it comes across a period.

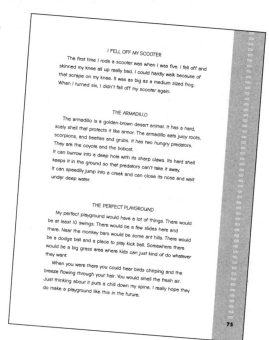

I FELL OFF MY SCOOTER

The first time I rode a scooter was when I was five. I fell off and skinned my knee all up really bad. I could hardly walk because of that scrape on my knee. It was as big as a medium sized frog. When I turned six, I didn't fall off my scooter again.

THE ARMADILLO

The armadillo is a golden-brown desert animal. It has a hard, scaly shell that protects it like armor. The armadillo eats juicy roots, scorpions, and beetles and grubs. It has two hungry predators. They are the coyote and the bobcat.
It can burrow into a deep hole with its sharp claws. Its hard shell keeps it in the ground so that predators can't take it away. It can speedily jump into a creek and can close its nose and wait under deep water.

THE PERFECT PLAYGROUND

My perfect playground would have a lot of things. There would be at least 10 swings. There would be a few slides here and there. Near the monkey bars would be some ant hills. There would be a dodge ball and a place to play kick ball. Somewhere there would be a big grass area where kids can just kind of do whatever they want.
When you were there you could hear birds chirping and the breeze flowing through your hair. You would smell the fresh air. Just thinking about it puts a chill down my spine. I really hope they do make a playground like this in the future.

75

I FELL OFF MY SCOOTER

The first time I rode a scooter was when I was five. I fell off and skinned my knee all up really bad. I could hardly walk because of that scrape on my knee. It was as big as a medium sized frog. When I turned six, I didn't fall off my scooter again.

THE ARMADILLO

The armadillo is a golden-brown desert animal. It has a hard, scaly shell that protects it like armor. The armadillo eats juicy roots, scorpions, and beetles and grubs. It has two hungry predators. They are the coyote and the bobcat.

It can burrow into a deep hole with its sharp claws. Its hard shell keeps it in the ground so that predators can't take it away. It can speedily jump into a creek and can close its nose and wait under deep water.

THE PERFECT PLAYGROUND

My perfect playground would have a lot of things. There would be at least 10 swings. There would be a few slides here and there. Near the monkey bars would be some ant hills. There would be a dodge ball and a place to play kick ball. Somewhere there would be a big grass area where kids can just kind of do whatever they want.

When you were there you could hear birds chirping and the breeze flowing through your hair. You would smell the fresh air. Just thinking about it puts a chill down my spine. I really hope they do make a playground like this in the future.

LESSON 19: PUNCTUATION WALKABOUT

Reread one of the passages aloud while simultaneously walking in a circle around the room. As you hit a period in your reading, abruptly stop reading and moving. Do this for several sentences. Then, explain that not only does your voice stop, but your feet also stop. Your voice (and feet) "walk" through sentences, but your voice (and feet) "stop" for periods.

Invite students to try the activity. First identify a path for students to walk around the classroom. Then, reread one of the passages. (You build students' confidence by letting them "walkabout" to a passage they've already heard you read multiple times.) As you read it aloud, be very deliberate with long pauses between sentences; get students to stop suddenly. Read the passage again, this time faster, making your period "stops" less deliberate. As students get better, increase your reading speed to a normal fluency and rate.

Read a second sample and repeat the activity. Keep reiterating that writers "hear" periods. Once students have mastered the writing samples, ask a volunteer to bring you a library book. Say: "Let's see if this works in books, too." Read aloud a section of the book, and have students walkabout, stopping for the periods they hear.

Finally, call on volunteers to share some of their own work from notebooks and journals. Say: "Let's see if this works in student writing. I'll read some of your work." Repeat the activity using one or two student samples.

NOTE If you would rather not have students walking around the classroom, try a "Punctuation Clapabout." As you read samples, have students clap once to signal periods they hear. Again, as they get better at the activity, increase your reading speed to a normal fluency and rate.

INDEPENDENT STUDENT WRITING ACTIVITY

Option 1: Have students read their pieces to themselves as they walk in a circle. When they hear themselves take a breath, tell them check for a period. They should add or remove punctuation, as necessary.

Option 2: Pair students. Have them take turns reading their pieces to their peers. The partner claps upon hearing a period (when the writer takes a breath). If he or she finds a spot where a period needs to be added or removed, the writer makes the change.

NOTE Have students read their pieces a couple times to themselves to build their reading fluency before reading aloud to partners. Otherwise, they might pause after every word while attempting to decode the phonics.

GROUP SHARE

Use this time to have students share how many "period" mistakes they found during writing time. Remind them that punctuation marks are tools writers use to help their readers. Readers need punctuation marks so they know where to breathe. Without them, the writers' ideas don't make sense.

LESSON EXTENSION

Create additional body gestures and movements for the "walkabout" to represent other punctuation marks, such as the following:

Periods: Stop and stomp your feet.

Exclamation points: Stop and jump.

Question marks: Stop and push up with your hands, palms up.

Read Up, Write Down

| LESSON RATIONALE | The kids in your class have heard you and previous teachers use the term "reread." For many students, the term simply means to look at every word from the top to bottom of the page. Since "rereading" has such a generic meaning, |

students tend to look at it as a busywork step in the writing process, rather than as an essential component. A three-step procedure for self-editing will help students be more deliberate in their rereading.

| LESSON TRIGGER | The physical shift from writer to reader will target your bodily-kinesthetic learners. |

Mini-Lesson

Explain to students that in order for writers to catch their own errors, they need to slow down during the "rereading" process. This can be done by following three key steps:

1. **READ UP, WRITE DOWN:** When writers draft, their paper is flat *down* on their desks. However, when editing, students should turn into readers by lifting their paper *up* off the writing surface. Thus, read "up" and write "down." By shifting from a writer's plane or perspective to a reader's plane, students will be able to correct more mistakes. (This is also true when the writer's plane is a 90-degree computer screen. If the writing is printed in hard-copy form and then shifted to a 45-degree reader's plane, more mistakes are caught.)

2. **WHISPER READING:** No one reads as fast out loud as he or she does silently. By reading aloud, students are forced to edit more slowly. (You might suggest they utilize whisper phone to keep the noise minimal.) Demonstrate how your lips are physically moving during a whisper reading. Caution students not to slide back into a silent reading after a few sentences.

3. TRACK WITH FINGER: As students are whisper reading, point out that sometimes we *think* we wrote a word that never made it onto the paper; our brains were moving faster than our pencils. By tracking each word with their index fingers as they read aloud, writers are more likely to spot those missing words.

NOTE There are hands-free whisper phones that allow students to amplify their voices, while keeping their hands available for holding up the writing and tracking with their fingers.

Have students pull out an old draft and practice the three key steps in editing. As they read up, write down, and whisper read, monitor that their lips are actually moving. Encourage them to track carefully—and not just go through the motions. Remind students that when they find an error, they should turn back into a writer by laying the piece down on the desk and making the change. Then, they should turn back into a reader (lift, whisper, track) and resume rereading.

This student is whisper reading while tracking with her finger.

This student is using a hands-free phone while holding his writing and tracking with his finger.

INDEPENDENT STUDENT WRITING ACTIVITY

Have students continue to practice the role of rereader as they edit previous writing.

LESSON EXTENSION

When students are comfortable with the three-step process, encourage them to edit for five different convention skills in five separate rereadings. With this type of focused editing, they are targeting one skill at a time. Skills might include the following:

1. Target only <u>capital letters</u> (beginning sentence, proper nouns, and so on).

2. Target only <u>punctuation marks</u> (end marks, middle-of-the-sentence marks, apostrophes, and so on).

3. Target only <u>spelling</u> (Word Wall words, big words spelled wrong, misspelled homophones, and so on).

4. Target only <u>paragraph indents</u> (upper grades) or <u>word spacing</u> (struggling writers).

5. Target a <u>current convention skill</u> you've been studying and want them to apply. (If you put each of these timely skills on a large sticky note, then you can change them frequently.)

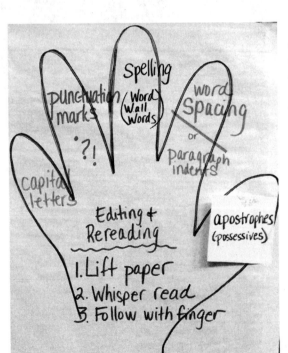

Assign a different colored pen to each editing skill. This increases student motivation to reread multiple times; they want to use the different colors. (Pen colors should correspond with the colored marker used on the wall chart.)

TRAIT-BASED WRITING